SIMPLE FLUTES

A Guide to Flute Making and Playing

or

How to Make and Play Simple Homemade Musical
Instruments from Bamboo, Wood, Clay, Metal,
PVC Plastic, or Anything Else

By Mark Shepard
Author of *How to Love Your Flute*

Simple Productions
Bellingham, Washington

Library of Congress subject headings:
Flute—Construction
Flute—Instruction and study

This book was first published by Simple Productions, Arcata,
California, 1992, and reprinted the same year by Tai Hei
Shakuhachi, Willits, California. This edition was first
published by Shepard Publications, Los Angeles, 2002.

Version 1.3

May we be made ever more perfect instruments.

Contents

1

Playing

You can play a flute! Simple flutes—from bamboo, wood, clay, metal, plastic, and other materials—not only sound beautiful, but they're easy, too.

For learning, a flute with six fingerholes is best. It should play a major scale in tune for two full octaves. With such a flute and the instructions here, you'll soon be playing simple songs.

The Sound

Getting a sound is easy!

Leave your fingers OFF the holes, for now. Rest your bottom lip on the edge of the mouthhole and blow it like a pop bottle.

Make sure the mouthhole is pointed directly upward and that you're holding your head straight up. Rest your bottom lip loosely on the edge—not pulled up, or curled under itself, or pressed down hard against the flute. Press your lips together at the corners, leaving a narrow opening at the front, centered on the mouthhole. Blow a solid stream of air directly at the opposite edge of the hole. Don't lift up your bottom lip as you blow!

If no sound comes, check your bottom lip to make sure you're not pulling it up. Then rotate the flute to change the angle at which your breath hits the edge. Also try varying the shape and pressure of your blowing. Looking in a mirror will help.

If your lips get tired, take a break. Don't worry if you feel dizzy. You just aren't used to breathing so deeply.

The Hands

Here is the best way to hold a standard six-hole flute. If your flute has more holes, or if it places them differently, you may have to change this a bit.

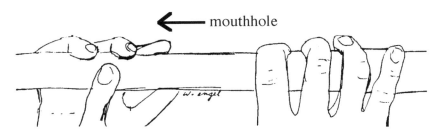

Your hands approach the flute from opposite sides. The holes are covered by the first three fingers of each hand. Your left hand comes in at an angle.

The flute is supported by

• your left index finger, curled under the flute in a "cradle."

• your left thumb, on the side of the flute, between the first and second fingerholes.

• your right thumb, under your right forefinger.

• one or both little fingers.

This will let you hold the flute securely with all fingers lifted from the holes. Never use your bottom lip to support the flute!

For best playing, keep your back straight, with your elbows and shoulders down. Tilt the flute slightly down and forward, keeping your head at right angles to the flute.

The Notes

Again lift your fingers from the holes. Blow the flute, and at the same time cover the first fingerhole (the one nearest the mouthhole). Cover it airtight with the fleshy face of your finger. You shouldn't need to press hard.

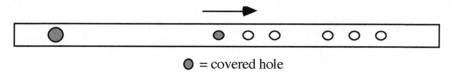

◒ = covered hole

If the note sounds good, keep that hole covered while you cover the next one. Keep covering more holes, as long as the notes sound good. Make sure you cover each hole completely. Each note should be lower.

As you play lower notes, your top lip should move slightly forward and down. Your lip opening should become larger and more relaxed.

If you lose the sound, or if it goes to a higher note, start over. Practice until you can play the lowest note, with all fingerholes covered.

This series of notes is called the "first octave."

Second Octave

To play the higher notes of the flute—the "second octave"—you will use the same fingerings, but blow differently.

Cover all the fingerholes. Narrow your lip opening and blow a little harder than before. You should hear a high note.

Now lift your fingers from the fingerholes, one at a time, starting with the *last* fingerhole (the one farthest from the mouthhole). Each note should be higher.

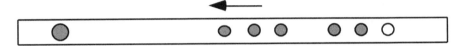

As you play higher notes, your upper lip should move up and back. Your lip opening should become narrower and tighter, making you blow harder to force your breath out.

When you've played the note that has all fingerholes uncovered, cover them all again and play the next higher note—the first note of the third octave.

The first note of both the second and third octave will usually sound better if you uncover the first fingerhole, as shown below.

Sharps and Flats

On a standard six-hole flute, playing the notes from lowest to highest should give you a major scale—*do, re, mi.* You should get a *minor* scale if you start with only the first fingerhole covered, then play higher, on into the second octave.

For many tunes, you won't need any other notes, if you find the right note to start on. But other tunes may call for sharps or flats—the "notes between the notes." You may also need sharps and flats while playing with other musicians.

Some flutes have extra holes to play these notes. Otherwise, there are two ways to play them. To "half-hole," cover only half of the last hole fingered.

To "cross-finger," uncover that same hole completely, but cover one or more holes below it.

Experiment to find the fingerings that work best for you.

Breath and Tonguing

With the tip of your tongue, add a light "t" to the beginning of individual notes or to the first note of a series.

You'll play better if you breathe deeply and correctly. To check this, place your hand on your stomach. As you inhale and your lungs expand, you should feel your stomach *push out*. Many people do the opposite, holding in their stomachs and breathing only with their upper chests.

Practice holding single notes long and steadily.

When your notes are fairly solid, you can also practice vibrato—a pulsing tone. Pull in your stomach in short jerks, as if belly-laughing. You can use vibrato to enhance long notes.

Making Music

When playing with other musicians, you can tune the flute slightly by rotating it so the mouthhole moves toward you or away. But the tone and the tuning of the notes to each other are best when you hold the flute normally.

To learn to play by ear, start with simple tunes, picking out the notes. Begin a tune on the note that lets you avoid sharps and flats, or that at least gives you the fewest.

To play written music, the simplest way is to transpose to the key of the flute. For example, when reading music written in the key of C major—as for soprano recorder— pretend that the flute too is in that key, and that its lowest note is C.

Flute Care

Flutes of bamboo or wood need special care. Unless the flute was coated inside with a hard finish, oil the inside occasionally with a food oil or light mineral oil. This prevents the flute from too quickly absorbing the moisture of playing, which can make it split. The flute can also split if it is brought suddenly into the cold, or if the flute is too cold when you play it.

The best guard against splitting is to bind the flute tightly with a strong cord, once below the mouthhole, and once at the flute's bottom end. (See the instructions under "Bamboo" in the next chapter.)

Plastic flutes can be cleaned with a scouring pad, or with bathroom cleanser or baking soda on a damp sponge.

Flute corks must be placed just right to bring the two octaves closely in tune with each other while giving a good tone. You may want to measure where your cork is, in case it gets moved. The cork must be airtight. If it gets loose, you can coat it with tallow, beeswax, or cork grease.

2

Making

Simple flutes can be made from almost any material that can form a tube. Some materials—like bamboo and plastic—are easy to start out on. Others—like wood, clay, and metal—require some experience.

Believe it or not, the material of the flute doesn't affect the sound nearly as much as the flute's measurements do. So, before dealing with materials, we'll discuss general guidelines for designing flutes.

Plan to make several flutes at least. Each one will be a bit better.

Flute Qualities

Here are some of the flute qualities we'll deal with:

Volume. How loud the flute can be played. We'll aim for a flute that can give us high volume when we need it.

Tone. The sound quality of the flute. We'll aim for a clear, "open" tone.

Range. The musical "distance" between the flute's low note and the highest note that can be played easily. We want a range of at least two octaves.

Octave tuning. The tuning of the flute's octaves to each other. If you play a note in the first octave of a simple flute, then the same note in the second octave, the two notes aren't likely to sound exactly in tune. The second note may be too high ("sharp"), or more likely too low ("flat"). But we want both notes to be close enough so we can "bend" them into tune as we play them.

The Flute Tube

The *length* of the tube roughly decides the flute's low note, which is also its "key." The longer the flute, the lower that note.

The table below shows rough tube lengths for the most popular flute keys. This measurement is for the flute interior only—in other words, from the open end of the tube, up to the stopper. The G flute will best serve the needs of most players.

The *inside diameter* (I.D.) of the tube—the distance between the tube walls—must vary with the length, for the sake of range and octave tuning. Longer tubes should be wider. For a simple flute, the best ratio of I.D. to length is about 1 to 23, or 4.35%. A wider tube than that will favor low notes, and a narrower tube will favor high notes. This measurement too is shown in the table.

The *wall thickness* of the tube is important mostly because it determines the depth of the fingerholes. A thin wall helps volume, tone, range, and octave tuning. Aim at 1/16 inch to 1/8 inch for most materials, and never thicker than 5/32 inch.

Key	Length	I.D.
G	16"	11/16" +
F	18"	3/4" +
E	19"	13/16" +
D	21"	7/8" +
C	23"	15/16" +

The Mouthhole

Thin tube walls are good for fingerholes, but a deeper mouthhole produces a more solid tone. On flutes of some materials, you can help this by forming a "lip plate," as on the modern flute.

A larger mouthhole will improve volume and tone. But a smaller mouthhole will improve range and octave tuning. A good compromise size is 7/16 inch or slightly larger. Even better is an oval of about the same area, for an edge better fitted to your blowing.

The mouthhole must be placed at just the right distance from the flute stopper to give the closest octave tuning, as well as a clear tone. A good beginning guess for this measurement is 2/3 of the flute tube's inside diameter—but you will have to experiment. (The distance is measured from the mouthhole center.)

The Fingerholes

Large fingerholes give better volume, tone, range, and octave tuning. But smaller holes are easier to cover, and also to reach, because they wind up closer together.

A good general hole size is 3/8 inch to 7/16 inch, depending on the flute's size and the player's fingers. But the holes don't need to be all the same size. Individual holes can be made as large as 1/2 inch, as long as you can reach and cover them.

The holes also don't need to be in a straight line. You may want to offset them to make fingering easier. On longer flutes, you could place the bottom hole under your little finger, instead of your ring finger, for better positioning and an easier reach.

Tuning

The notes of the flute are determined chiefly by the size and placement of the fingerholes.

The chart below gives a rough guide to where to put the holes. The chart's measurements are shown as percentages of distance from the mouthhole. All measurements are from hole centers, not edges.

The chart provides a starting point only. From there, you will have to experiment with final placement and hole size, using the tuning techniques we'll now discuss.

Here are the two most important rules for tuning:

• A hole will give a higher note if it is placed closer to the mouthhole. It will give a lower note if placed farther away.
• A hole will give a higher note if made larger. It will give a lower note if smaller.

These rules mean you can "raise" a note by enlarging the hole *or* by placing the hole closer to the mouthhole. You can "lower" the note by using a smaller hole *or* by placing the hole farther from the mouthhole.

It also means you can change the hole size *and* its placement *without* changing the note. A larger hole could be placed farther from the mouthhole, or a smaller hole placed closer to the mouthhole.

The tuning of any fingerhole's note is also affected by:

- The depth of the hole—in other words, the thickness of the tube. The deeper the hole, the lower the note.
- The open fingerholes farther from the mouthhole. The more and larger these fingerholes, the higher the note.
- The size and depth of the mouthhole. The larger the mouthhole, the higher the note. The deeper the mouthhole, the lower the note.
- The placement of the stopper. The closer to the mouthhole, the higher the note.
- The width of the tube. A wider tube produces a lower note.

Generally, anything that "opens up" the tube wall and allows the air to vibrate more freely will raise the note. Anything that "closes" the wall and resists air vibration will lower it.

How you play the flute will also affect the tuning. When checking the tuning of a note, play at a medium loudness, with your fingers at a medium height over the fingerholes, and without bending over the mouthhole. Try your best not to "bend" the notes into tune, as you would during normal playing.

Also keep in mind that the first note in both the second and third octave is fingered differently from the flute's low note. Instead of covering all the holes, you should leave the top hole uncovered as a "vent," as shown below.

The tuning of these two higher notes is affected by both the flute length and the size of the vent hole. Enlarging the vent hole or placing it closer to the mouthhole will sharpen the first note of the second octave. It will *flatten* the first note of the *third* octave.

For tuning, the notes of the flute can be compared to the notes of a piano, pitchpipe, or other tuning instrument. Play your own note first, so you aren't tempted to "bend" your note to match the other.

Or you can simply tune the notes of the flute to each other, in the *do-re-mi* pattern, with the low note as *do*. If you tune this way, check each note against the flute's low note, so you don't "drift" out of tune.

Whichever way you choose, remember that the notes of the flute aren't supposed to be *exactly* in tune, but only close enough to "bend" into tune when you play them. This is because simple flutes seldom have perfect octave tuning.

To make sure both the first and the second octave are tuned well enough, the first octave must normally be tuned a little sharp, and the second octave a little flat. You may also have to smooth out differences in "out-of-tuneness" between holes of different sizes.

Tuning is the chief art in simple flutemaking. It will become easier, and you'll get better, the more you do it.

Stoppers

Flutes of some materials—like bamboo and clay—are easily made with built-in stopped ends. But many flutes instead have separate stoppers.

The most common stopper is straight-sided (untapered) cork. Possible sources for new cork are hardware stores, music stores, and brewery supply outlets. Try the Yellow Pages of your phone directory. If you can't find the right size or shape, you can trim or sand down a larger cork—preferably on a lathe, to keep it even. To cut cork by hand, use a fresh razor blade.

The cork *must* be airtight. In fact, it should start out extra tight, since it will shrink with age. To insert a tight cork, lubricate it with cork grease or plain water.

If you can't use cork, any stopper will do, as long as it's airtight. If you glue a stopper in place, be sure to use waterproof glue.

Finishes

Bamboo and wood require finishes, inside and out, to resist moisture and guard against cracking. You have many choices.

Wooden orchestra instruments are finished with bore oil, which is nothing but light mineral oil. Be careful not to use too much on the outside of your flute, because it never dries! Almond oil is used by many flutemakers. Buy it at a natural foods store. If you prefer an oil that dries, you can use walnut oil.

Avoid using commercial finishes from hardware stores on the outside of your flute, because they almost always have toxic additives. However, they work well *inside,* sealing against moisture better than most natural finishes. One way to apply a finish inside only is to seal the flute holes with masking tape and pour in the finish.

Other options for the outside include shellac and petroleum jelly. Organic wood finishes are sometimes advertised in fine woodworking magazines.

Plastic

Plastic plumbing pipe is nearly ideal for simple flutes. There's no easier material to work with. Sanded clean and smooth, it's attractive, requiring no finish. It's waterproof, crack-proof, and nearly unbreakable. It's fine acoustically, if you use the right dimensions. And once you develop a pattern, the pipe's regularity allows a perfect flute every time.

The plastic we're talking about is PVC (polyvinyl chloride), used for cold water supply, and its close cousin CPVC (chloro-polyvinyl chloride), for hot water. DO NOT use ABS pipe for flutes. Since it's meant only for drainage, there are no restrictions on the toxicity of the chemicals added to it. Also avoid gray PVC electrical conduit, both because of possible toxicity and because of its greater wall thickness, which will hurt octave tuning.

Plastic pipe can be cut just like wood, though it dulls your tools more quickly. For drilling, use a very slow speed to minimize "grabbing" when the bit reaches the interior. Or avoid the grabbing entirely with "zero-rake" drill bits. You can order these specially or else modify regular twist drill bits by grinding. Find instructions for this in books on tools and sharpening. Don't use flat bits—the size of the holes they make is not accurate.

After drilling, stick a long wood dowel into the tube to break loose the plastic "shavings" hanging inside. Smooth all hole edges and end edges with a narrow, very sharp knife blade or an apple peeler. If there's too much hiss later when you play the flute, this may mean the mouthhole edge is too sharp.

Sand the tube at a sink, keeping the tube wet and using wet-and-dry sandpaper. This lets you rinse off your sandpaper as it clogs, and it also stops the dust from flying. (You don't want this dust in your lungs. It never decomposes! If you "dry sand," at least use a dust mask.) A heavy-duty scouring pad will also work, with some patience. Clean the inside with a bottle brush and water.

A good trick is to use a plumbing pipe end cap—a standard part—as a combination stopper and lip plate. Glue it on with plastic pipe cement, then drill the mouthhole through it. Apply the cement to the pipe surface only—not inside the cap—to avoid pushing the excess into the flute, where fumes can persist much longer. A flute made in this fashion should remain playable for thousands of years!

Use a different arrangement for pipe that is 1 inch or wider, so you can move the mouthhole farther from the end. At the top end of the pipe, place a slip coupling—a standard part used to join two lengths of pipe. Seal the opposite end of the coupling with a spigot plug. Again, always apply pipe cement so it's pushed out of the joint, not in. Then drill the mouthhole through the slip coupling.

If you prefer a different way to stop the pipe, you can choose to do without a lip plate, but having one does improve the acoustics. One way to make one separately is to cut the pipe at your mouthhole mark and glue both pieces into a slip coupling. Or you can file the internal ridge out of a slip coupling and glue it over an intact length of pipe. If you don't want the pipe completely surrounded by this coupling, you can first cut away some of its circumference.

A slip coupling can be used also as a tuning slide. After drilling your holes, cut away a tiny section of pipe between mouthhole and first fingerhole, then glue the coupling to one cut end. Be aware, though, that any arrangement with moving parts is likely to cause trouble as parts wear down.

Plumbing pipe flutes pick up dirt easily—an especial problem with white pipe. But you can easily clean them with a scouring pad, or with baking soda or bathroom cleanser on a damp sponge.

Mild fumes migrate out of plastic pipe for long after it leaves the factory, especially when heated by tools. If you make a lot of flutes over a long period, breathing these fumes *could* harm you—so work only with good ventilation. Pipe cement is much worse still, so you might want to use it outdoors. And don't play a flute with a cemented part until the cement has completely dried. You can help this along by leaving the piece in direct sunlight or by a heating vent.

Following is the plan for a flute I designed in the summer of 1988. I call it the "Plumber's Pipe." It's in the key of G and plays two full octaves. Of course, you might have to modify the design, depending on materials available to you.

The Plumber's Pipe

Hole Size

$^7/_{16}"$ Rotate 25° up: $^3/_8"$ $^3/_8"$ $^3/_8"$ Rotate 10° up: $^{11}/_{32}"$ $^7/_{16}"$ $^5/_{16}"$

$^5/_{16}"$ $6^7/_8"$ $8"$ $9^1/_8"$ $10^3/_4"$ $11^1/_2"$ $12^3/_4"$ $15^9/_{16}"$

Hole Distance

The flute is made from 3/4 inch CPVC pipe, plus a standard end cap. The actual exact dimensions of the pipe are 7/8 inch outside diameter, 11/16 inch inside diameter, 3/32 inch wall thickness. The tube length, with the end cap *off*, is 15 $^9/_{16}$ inches. The wall thickness of the end cap too is 3/32 inch, for a total mouthhole depth of 3/16 inch.

The chart shows the size of each hole and the distance from its center to the top of the flute tube—again, measured with the flute cap *off*. You can mark these distances on a piece of paper, a ruler, a dowel, or a length of pipe, then use this pattern to help place the holes on your pipe. Two holes are slightly offset as shown, for easier fingering.

There is no copyright or patent on this design. Feel free to make as many as you like, and to sell them too!

Bamboo

Bamboo almost begs to be made into flutes. So it's no wonder that bamboo is the flute material of choice in many parts of the world.

Find commercial Taiwan bamboo in Oriental gift shops, import outlets, hardware stores, and specialty furniture manufacturers. Check the Yellow Pages. You might also like to try local bamboo, but not all kinds will have decent octave tuning. Harvested bamboo needs to season in a cool place for nine months before use.

In the U.S., the best commercial bamboo size for flute-making is called "inch and a quarter," based on diameter at the root end. But sometimes this same size is called "inch and a half," though it's really not. In some areas, you won't find this size at all, and you must content yourself with the thickest pieces from the "one inch" category and the thinnest pieces from "one and a half."

Bamboo poles of this diameter come in lengths up to 15 feet. However, only the mid-section is good for the kind of flutes described here. Shorter poles of this diameter are shorter only because the thin, unusable top has been cut off.

Look at the overall condition of the bamboo. Select pieces with long joints, for better octave tuning. Check carefully for cracks—especially tiny ones at the nodes—and for small holes. Choose the pieces with the fewest flaws. A curve is no problem.

Bamboo is a series of hollow compartments, separated by walls at the nodes. Each flute piece you cut from your pole should include a node wall to act as the flute stopper, plus a length of bamboo measured from that node. If the piece includes other node walls, you will be removing them.

Use the table of lengths and widths given earlier to plan your cuts. You can cut at any distance above the stopper node at the flute top, but about 1 inch is convenient and looks good. Avoid including even tiny cracks (except maybe above the stopper node) because they are sure to expand.

For better octave tuning, cut your flute piece so there's no more than one node to hollow. Also, don't use pieces with a wall thickness over 5/32 inch. The thick-walled root end is better used for shakuhachis—Japanese end-blown flutes. (See "Resources" in the back of this book.)

Cut your bamboo with a fine-toothed blade, to avoid splintering. For instance, you could use a metal-cutting hacksaw with a miter box.

Remove unwanted node walls as completely as possible, for the sake of octave tuning. One way is to punch them out with a long rod, or drill them with an auger bit, then rasp down the edges. "Dragon skin" wrapped around a dowel is one rasping tool. A quick, clean way to remove the walls is with an electric drill, a drill bit extension, and a set of flat bits. Wear a kitchen mitt, hold the node that's being drilled, and avoid overheating.

A common way, not as efficient, is to burn out the walls with a metal rod or tube heated over a flame. But only do this out of doors or with excellent ventilation, because the smoke can seriously irritate your lungs.

Cut and hollow your pieces as soon as possible after purchase, to avoid further cracking.

The commonest way to make bamboo flute holes is by burning. This allows quick and easy enlargement of individual holes for custom tuning.

You can use a piece of metal rod with a pointed or flat end, heated over a flame. For instance, you could use a drill bit held in a file handle, heated by a torch. Another possibility is an electric soldering iron, held with a kitchen mitt.

Normally, you will make the mouthhole first. Burn through the flute wall, then expand the hole by pressing your tool against the sides. An oval hole gives a better blowing edge. At this point, you can check the flute's low note, and adjust the flute's length if necessary.

Next, make and tune each fingerhole in turn. Start from the bottom—the end opposite the mouthhole—because each hole affects the ones above. Check each note against the flute's low note, to avoid drifting off tune. Remember that you are tuning the second-octave note, as well!

If a hole is getting too big, you can sharpen it further by angling your tool to enlarge the hole on the inside only. A hole made too big can be made smaller again with epoxy around the edge.

Fingerholes too can be oval, allowing easy covering of larger holes. Expand them in line with approaching fingers.

Again, TRY NOT TO BREATHE THE SMOKE. In fact, if you're sensitive to smoke, don't burn bamboo at all.

You may prefer to drill the holes. You can use regular drill bits at a very slow speed, but "zero-rake" drill bits will prevent grabbing and splitting. You can order these bits specially—they're normally used for plastics—but it's cheaper to regrind the rake angle of regular twist drill bits. Find instructions in books on tools and sharpening. You will have to take care not to overheat these bits.

Bamboo needs only a light sanding, to remove dirt. A bottle brush will clean the inside.

You can decorate the flute by burning in an insignia, or running a torch over it to darken it, or even by inlaying.

A bamboo flute will crack and split when the inside of the tube expands much more rapidly than the outside. This can happen when you take a flute outside on a cold day and blow your warm breath into it. It can also happen anytime the flute absorbs moisture from your breath too quickly. To resist moisture and guard against cracking, bamboo requires finishes inside and out. (See the discussion of finishes given earlier.)

You should also bind the flute, at least once below the mouthhole and once at the open end. See the illustration following. You can't pull the cord tight enough with your fingers alone, so use one or more dowels, sticks, or extra bamboo pieces for wrapping, pulling, and levering. The finished binding must be tight enough that the end loops don't spread out when you nudge them with a finger.

You can find a wide variety of cords for binding at hardware stores and craft shops. Your cord must be strong, not slippery, and attractive. One favorite is waxed flax (linen). Another is waxed nylon, available from leather supply and shoe repair shops.

Synthetic cords become tighter and stronger when the air is dry. Natural cords become tighter and stronger when the air is humid—but hot, humid weather also shortens their life. Waxed cords aren't as affected by changes in humidity, and last longer. Among natural fibers, cotton and jute are too weak.

You can make your bindings even stronger by coating them with epoxy or melted wax.

Binding a Flute

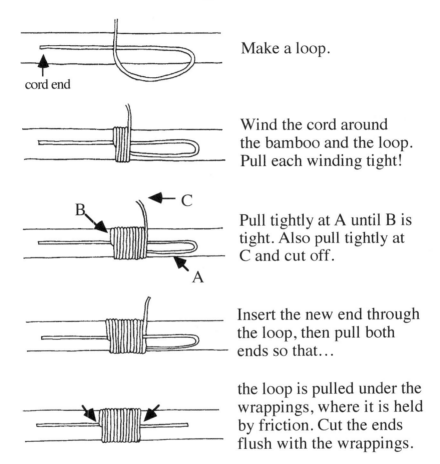

Make a loop.

cord end

Wind the cord around
the bamboo and the loop.
Pull each winding tight!

Pull tightly at A until B is
tight. Also pull tightly at
C and cut off.

Insert the new end through
the loop, then pull both
ends so that...

the loop is pulled under the
wrappings, where it is held
by friction. Cut the ends
flush with the wrappings.

To repair a flute already cracked, pull the crack together
with a motor hose band, available at hardware and automo-
tive stores. Bind the flute, then remove the band. You won't
need glue or filler in the crack.

Wood

Wood is one of the finest materials for flutemaking, because of the exactness with which it can be worked. Before this century, most flutes in European cultures were made from wood. This has been a special art of the experienced woodturner.

Wood for flutes must be hard, fine-grained, and non-toxic. Maple is good, and so are fruit woods like cherry. In general, look for light-colored, heavy woods, without visible pores.

Dark woods are dark because they're loaded with toxins to resist decay. These woods can irritate the skin of players sensitive to them, and the inhaled dust can cause serious health problems for the maker. If in doubt, *taste* the wood. Non-toxic woods have almost no taste. If you do work with toxic wood, be sure to use a good exhaust system or wear a dust mask approved for toxic dust. (The masks don't work as well with a beard!)

Some flutemakers use tropical woods like rosewood. Be aware that these are *extremely* toxic to some players. Using such wood in quantity may also contribute to deforestation of tropical rain forests.

Another material you might consider, which is worked much like wood, is ebonite. This is a synthetic rubber used today for almost all student-model woodwinds. It's waterproof and won't crack, so it's much less touchy than wood. R. S. Rockstro, the pre-eminent nineteenth-century authority on the flute, proclaimed it the ideal flute material! Ebonite is not considered toxic, but you'll need to carefully protect yourself from inhaling the dust, because your body cannot break it down.

For wood pieces, buy well-seasoned 1 $1/2$-inch or 2-inch lumber, then cut your flute blanks on a bandsaw. Better yet is to split the wood, to avoid warping in the finished flute. Discard any pieces with checks.

Start making your blank into a flute by placing it on your lathe and rough-turning it to a cylinder.

The second step is the most specialized: making the bore. To avoid drifting off-center, you'll need a shell auger. These were once readily available from fine woodworking tool suppliers, but now can be hard to find. (As of 2000, shell augers were being made and sold by Vanguard Cutting Tools, 102 Harvest Lane, Sheffield S3 8EG, England, +44-0-114-273-7677.) In a pinch, you can have one custom-made by a machine shop—or if you can work metal yourself, you can make your own. Plans are in Trevor Robinson's *The Amateur Wind Instrument Maker*.

Even better than a shell auger is a gun drill—but it costs much more and requires compressed air.

You'll also need a three-point steady to hold the end being bored, or else a "hollow tailstock" you can feed the auger through. You can make a simple one from a copper plumping pipe T-fitting with one end sharpened, fastened in your tool rest base. A better one could be devised using a ball bearing. At the headstock, a three-jaw chuck is best.

First make a short pilot hole, using a twist drill in a tailstock chuck. Then remove the regular tailstock and hand-feed the shell auger. The shell auger is self-centering, so you don't have to worry about aligning it. Remove the auger now and then to clear chips and prevent overheating. Be careful not to push the auger to the live center!

Once the shell auger has made a pilot bore, you can enlarge it to size with a twist drill bit, a homemade flat bit, or other.

One advantage of woodturning flutes is that you can easily modify the bore to change the acoustics. For instance, you could imitate the taper found in the headjoints of modern flutes, which greatly improves octave tuning. Roughly, this is a 10% reduction of the inside diameter over the top fifth of the flute interior (ending at the stopper). You can make a simple reamer to create this taper, by grinding a file.

When you've completed the bore, finish turn the outside, supporting one or both ends on a tapered mandrel. You may want to leave extra diameter where the mouthhole will be, so you can carve a lip plate.

Next drill the fingerholes, inserting a dowel in the bore to avoid tearout. If you're tuning a flute individually, start with small holes and gradually enlarge them.

Round files can be used to shape the mouthhole or undercut the fingerholes. You can sharpen a second-octave note alone by slightly enlarging the bore at the *antinode,* the point about halfway between the mouthhole and the fingerhole.

Now sand the flute on the lathe. To sand the bore, saw a slit in one end of a dowel, then slip in sanding paper and wrap it around the dowel. Don't worry about rounding the mouthhole and fingerhole edges slightly—this makes them more comfortable and even reduces hiss at the mouthhole.

You're then ready to finish the flute and install the stopper, if you need one. See the earlier sections on this.

Wood flutes can get much fancier. For instance, you could make decorative turnings on the outside. Or you could made the flute in two sections, connected by a cork-covered tenon, to allow tuning by moving the headjoint in or out. For these and other possibilities, see the books listed in the back in "Resources."

Clay

Beautiful flutes can be made of porcelain, earthenware, or stoneware. The process used most often is slip casting.

First make a plaster mold. For the male mold, use a pipe or tube with the outside diameter you want. Lubricate this piece so you can more easily get it out.

As soon as the plaster becomes solid, pull out the male mold. It won't be easy! Try first pouring cold water inside to contract it.

When the plaster has dried, pour in your clay slip, and let it set on the mold wall to the thickness you want. Drain the left-over slip, and let the cast dry for up to a day. It will shrink from the mold so you can remove it.

Make your flute while the clay is still only leather-hard. Drill your holes with twist drill bits. You can expand a hole with a larger bit if you first countersink the hole, to avoid chipping of the edge. Of course, you must handle the tube very carefully.

Let the flute dry completely before firing. You can then sand the flute with wet-and-dry sandpaper.

Glazing can be beautiful, but may alter the hole size. You could instead vitrify the flute with a high-firing.

Metal

When we think of metal flutes, we usually think of the modern flute. But metal is used for simple flutes as well. Steel, bronze, and aluminum are possible materials. You could also electroplate the flute with nickel or silver, as is done on student flutes.

Use only hardened metals. Soft metals such as you get from hardware stores and plumbing suppliers will rub off easily and can poison the player. Plating the metal will only delay this till the plating wears off.

If you work in metal, you might try some of the tricks used in modern flutes. A lip plate could be soldered to the flute tube. The top fifth of the tube (below the stopper) could be tapered 10% to improve the octave tuning. The flute could be made in two pieces with a tight sliding fit, so the top can be pulled in or out to slightly tune the flute.

Other

Don't think we've covered all the possibilities! Have you ever seen a glass flute? Or one from a sunflower stalk? I have! So use your imagination and see what you come up with.

Resources

For updated info and other materials, check Mark Shepard's Flute Page at www.markshep.com/flute.

In my book *How to Love Your Flute: A Guide to Flutes and Flute Playing,* you'll find instructions for selecting, playing, and caring for modern and simple flutes. You'll also find background information on flute history, flutes around the world, and flute acoustics.

Tai Hei Shakuhachi carries a comprehensive collection of books on flutemaking. Contact them at P.O. Box 294, Willits, CA 95490, 707-459-3402, monty@shakuhachi.com, www.shakuhachi.com.

Practical guidance on flutemaking can be found in scattered articles in craft magazines, project books, and books on making various musical instruments. Books and articles on acoustics and flute history are often helpful, as well. Your library is a good place to search.

To all serious flutemakers, I recommend *The Flute and Flute-Playing,* by Theobald Boehm, Dover, New York, 1964 (reprint). This is a major work by the inventor of the modern flute. My other favorite is *The Flute,* by Philip Bate, Benn, London, and Norton, New York, 1979. Woodturners may want to look at *The Amateur Wind Instrument Maker,* by Trevor Robinson, University of Massachusetts, Amherst, 1973.

About the Author

Mark Shepard is the author of *How to Love Your Flute: A Guide to Flutes and Flute Playing,* called by Paul Horn "a model for our times." He was a professional flutist and simple flutemaker for many years. Visit him at

www.markshep.com/flute

CPSIA information can be obtained
at www.ICGtesting.com
Printed in the USA
BVHW041029181220
595610BV00015B/551